Bush Theatre

T0347314

LEAVE TAKING

by Winsome Pinnock

24 May–30 June 2018
Bush Theatre, London

LEAVE TAKING

by Winsome Pinnock

Cast

Mai	**Adjoa Andoh**
Del	**Seraphina Beh**
Viv	**Nicholle Cherrie**
Brod	**Wil Johnson**
Enid	**Sarah Niles**

Director	**Madani Younis**
Associate Director	**Omar Elerian**
Designer	**Rosanna Vize**
Lighting Designer	**Rajiv Pattani**
Sound Designer	**Ed Clarke**
Production Manager	**Michael Ager**
Company Stage Manager	**Eleanor Dear**
Deputy Stage Manager	**Hanne Schulpé**

CAST

Adjoa Andoh Mai

Adjoa is making her Bush Theatre debut in *Leave Taking*. Previous theatre includes: *Julius Caesar* (Bridge Theatre); *Assata Taught Me* (Gate Theatre); *Soul* (Royal & Derngate/Hackney Empire); *Les Liaisons Dangereuses* (Donmar Warehouse); *Wolf in Snakeskin Shoes, Starstruck* (Tricycle Theatre); *Great Expectations* (Bristol Old Vic); *Julius Caesar, Tamburlaine, The Odyssey* (RSC), *Or You Could Kiss Me, His Dark Materials, Stuff Happens, The Revenger's Tragedy* (National Theatre); *Blood Wedding* (Almeida Theatre); *Joe Turner's Come and Gone, In The Red And Brown Water, The Snow Queen* (Young Vic); *Breath Boom, Sugar Mummies* (Royal Court); *Purgatorio* (Arcola Theatre); *Nights at the Circus* (Kneehigh/Lyric Hammersmith) *Pericles* (Lyric Hammersmith); *The Dispute* (RSC/Lyric Hammersmith); *Glory* (Lyric Hammersmith/Derby Playhouse/West Yorkshire Playhouse); *In The Bunker With The Ladies* (Drill Hall); *The Vagina Monologues* (Criterion/tour); *Death Catches the Hunter* (Traverse Theatre/Wild Iris); *Love at A Loss* (Wild Iris/ BAC/UK tour); *Cloud Nine* (Contact); *Our Day Out* (Birmingham Rep); *Princhdice and Co, Lear's Daughters* (Women's Theatre Group).

Her film credits include: *Brotherhood, Remainder, Julius Caesar, Invictus, Adulthood, Every Time I Look at You, A Rather English Marriage, I Is a Long Married Woman, What My Mother Told Me, The Missing Finger, One in Four A Short Film About Melons.* Television includes: *Death in Paradise, Acceptable Risk, Liar, Cucumber, Chasing Shadows, Law & Order, Line of Duty, New Tricks, River, The Interceptor, Missing, Scott and Bailey, Wire in the Blood, MI High, Doctor Who, The Shadow in the North, Chopra Town, Silent Witness, Dalziel & Pascoe, Casualty, In Search of Myths and Heroes, Brian Pern: Death of Rock, Wizards vs Aliens, Grandpa in My Pocket, Mrs. Inbetweeny, Macbeth, Jonathan Creek, Close Relations, An Independent Man, Health and Efficiency, The Brittas Empire, Peak Practice, Thieftakers, Tomorrow People, Circle of Deceit, Twelve Angry Men, Brass Eye, Birthrights, West Indian Women at War.*

Seraphina Beh Del

Serapina recently appeared in the Bush Theatre and Royal Exchange Theatre's production of *Parliament Square.* Her other theatre credits include: *Pigeon English, Romeo and Juliet, DNA* (National Youth Theatre); *Cosmic Jives* (Albany Theatre); *Black Attack* (Bush Theatre); *My Beautiful City* (Arcola Theatre); *Jack and the Beanstalk* (Lyric Hammersmith); *Ondisting, Romeo and Juliet Et Al, Skeen* (Ovalhouse Theatre). Television credits include: *EastEnders, Casualty* (BBC); *Game Face* (Objective Productions); *Live At The Electric* (Avalon Television).

Nicholle Cherrie Viv

Nicholle is a recent graduate of Arts Ed. Her theatre credits include: *Mamma Mia* (Cyprus) in the role of Lisa and *Jesus Christ Superstar* (Regent's Park Open Air Theatre). Whilst in training her credits include: *The Life, The Mystery of Edwin Drood, Hayfever* (Arts Ed), Olivier Awards 2016 (Royal Opera House), *Olympia Horse Show 2015* (The Grand Hall, Olympia), *My Lifelong Love* (Garrick Theatre).

Wil Johnson Brod

Wil makes his Bush Theatre debut in *Leave Taking*. His credits as a stage actor include: *Rosencrantz & Guildenstern Are Dead* (Old Vic); *King Lear* (Royal Exchange Theatre, Manchester); *A Wolf In Snakeskin Shoes* (Tricycle Theatre); *Fuente Ovejuna* (National Theatre); *Redundant* (Royal Court); *A Mad World My Masters* (Shakespeare's Globe); *Serious Money* (Birmingham Rep); *The Queen and I* (Out of Joint); *Torn* (Arcola Theatre) and the lead in *Othello* (Royal Lyceum). TV credits include: *Carnival Row* (Legendary); *Outlander* (Starz/Amazon); *Vera, Lewis* (ITV); *Waking the Dead* (BBC); *The Five* and *Clocking Off* (Red Productions); *Moving On* (LA Productions) and BAFTA Best Drama series, *Cracker* (Granada Television); *Hidden Treasure* (BAFTA Best Drama). Wil has also appeared in *Waterloo Road* (Shed Production); *Hollyoaks* (C4) and *Emmerdale* (ITV Yorkshire). Wil's film credits include: *Adulthood* (Adulthood ltd); *Anuvahood* (Revolver); *Midnight Breaks* (Film 4); *Dead End* (Oceanstorm films) and *Macbeth* (Green Screen Productions).

Sarah Niles Enid

Sarah last appeared at the Bush Theatre in *The Interrogation of Sandra Bland* as part of *Black Lives, Black Words*. Her theatre credits include: *B, The Sewing Group, Father Comes Home From The Wars* (Parts 1, 2 & 3); *Truth & Reconciliation* (Royal Court); *Boy* (Almeida Theatre); *The Crucible* (Old Vic); *Anthony & Cleopatra* (RSC/Off Broadway); *Table, Mrs Affleck* (National Theatre); *A Question of Freedom* (Feelgood); *The Long Road* (Curve, Leicester); *The Quiet Little Englishman* (Zho Visual); *Play Size* (ATC/Young Vic); *Bones* (Bush Theatre); *The Bogus Woman, The Lion the Witch and the Wardrobe, To Kill a Mockingbird* (Haymarket, Leicester); *Entarete Musik* (Amazonia Theatre Company); *Lowdown High Notes* (Red Ladder); *Black Love* (Black Arts Development Project); *Caucasian Chalk Circle* (Manchester Library). Television credits include: *Moving On, Death in Paradise, Waterloo Road, Being Human, Beautiful People, Doctor Who, Don't Take My Baby* (BBC); *Catastrophe* (Channel 4); *Spotless* (Netflix); *Marley's Ghosts* (UKTV); *Lucky Man* (Sky); *Thorne: Sleepyhead* (Sky); *Mister Eleven, A Touch of Frost* (ITV). Film credits include: *Still, Austenland, Cuban Fury, Now Is Good, London Boulevard, Games Men Play, Happy-Go-Lucky*.

CREATIVES

Winsome Pinnock Playwright
Winsome is a playwright and academic who was born in London to parents who were both migrants from Jamaica.

Her theatre credits include: *The Principles of Cartography* (Bush Theatre); *Tituba* (Hampstead Theatre); *Cleaning Up*, *Taken* (Clean Break at Ovalhouse Theatre); *IDP, One Under, Water* (Tricycle Theatre); *The Stowaway* (Plymouth Theatre); *Beg Borrow or Steal* (Kuumba Community Arts Centre); *Mules, Water, A Hero's Welcome, A Rock in Water* (Royal Court); *Can you Keep a Secret?* (NT Connections); *Leave Taking* (Liverpool Playhouse Theatre); *The Wind of Change* (Half Moon Theatre); *Picture Palace* (Women's Theatre Group). Radio plays include: *Clean Trade* (Radio 4); *Lazarus* (BBC Radio 3); *Her Father's Daughter* (BBC Radio 4); *Let Them Call it Jazz* (adapted from Jean Rhys' short story, BBC Radio 4); *Indiana* (adapted from novel by George Sand); *The Dinner Party* (BBC Radio 4); *Something Borrowed* (BBC Radio 4) and *Water* (BBC Radio 4). She co-wrote the screenplay *Bitter Harvest*.

Awards include: the George Devine Award, Pearson Plays on Stage Scheme best play of the year Award, Unity Trust Theatre Award. She was also runner-up for the Susan Smith Blackburn Prize. She was Senior Visiting Fellow at Cambridge University and writer in residence at Holloway Prison, Clean Break Theatre Company, Royal Court Theatre, Kuumba Arts Community Centre, Tricycle Theatre, and the National Theatre Studio. She is currently Associate Professor at Kingston University.

Madani Younis Director
Madani took over as Artistic Director of the Bush Theatre in 2012. He directed the critically acclaimed UK premiere of *The Royale* in 2015 which was revived in 2016. In 2013 he won the Groucho Club Maverick Award for the theatre, following the most successful season in the theatre's history which played to 99% capacity. Also for the Bush Theatre he has directed *The Principles of Cartography* as part of *Black Lives, Black Words, Zaida and Aadam* as part of *This Place We Know*, *Perseverance Drive* and *Chalet Lines*.

Madani is currently working as a member of the Mayor of London's Cultural Board.

Prior to his appointment at the Bush Theatre, he was Artistic Director of Freedom Studios in Bradford, Yorkshire where his work included the site-specific work, *The Mill – City of Dreams*. He has also worked nationally and internationally as a theatre director, writer and practitioner. He was previously Director of Red Ladder Theatre Company's Asian Theatre School where he directed *Silent Cry*, *Free World* and *Streets of Rope*.

He originally trained in film, and his debut short film *Ellabellapumpanella*, commissioned by the UK Film Council, was screened at the Cannes Film Festival in May 2007. He was the recipient of the Decibel Award at the South Bank Awards show in 2006.

Omar Elerian Associate Director

Omar is an award-winning Italian/Palestinian theatre director, deviser and performer, who trained at Jacques Lecoq International Theatre School in Paris. He joined the Bush in 2012 alongside Madani Younis and since then has been the resident Associate Director. He is in charge of the Bush's talent development, leading on the Associate Artists and Project 2036 schemes. He is also involved in the development and delivery of the Bush's artistic program and led the programming of the RADAR festival between 2012 and 2015. His directing credits for the Bush include gig theatre sensation *Misty* by Arinzé Kene, the Edinburgh Fringe First winning *NASSIM* by Nassim Soleimanpour, *One Cold Dark Night* by Nancy Harris and *Islands* by Caroline Horton. As Associate Director, he has worked alongside Madani Younis on the Bush's productions of *The Royale*, *Perseverance Drive* and *Chalet Lines*. Other credits include acclaimed site-specific production *The Mill – City of Dreams*, Olivier Award nominated *You're Not Like The Other Girls Chrissy*, *Testa di Rame* (Italy), *Les P'tites Grandes Choses* (France) and *L'Envers du Décor* (France).

Rosanna Vize Designer

Rosanna trained at Bristol Old Vic Theatre School as a theatre designer. She has worked regularly as an assistant to Anna Fleischle and was the resident design assistant for the RSC from September 2014 to September 2015. She was a Linbury Prize Finalist in 2013 working with English Touring Opera and is currently one of the Jerwood Young Designers.

Theatre includes: *King Lear* (Shakespeare's Globe, dir: Nancy Meckler); *The Earthworks & Myth* (RSC); *The Almighty Sometimes* (Royal Exchange Theatre, Manchester); *Yous Two* and *The Phlebotomist* (Hampstead Theatre); *Henry I* (Reading Between the Lines); *Girls* (Soho Theatre/Hightide/Talawa Theatre); *FUP, Noye's Fludde* (Kneehigh Theatre); *Dark Land Lighthouse, St Joan of the Stockyards, A Thousand Seasons Passed, The Tinder Box, The Last Days of Mankind, Talon* (Bristol Old Vic); *Diary of a Madman, The Rise and Shine of Comrade Fiasco* (Gate Theatre); *Infinite Lives, Coastal Defenses* (Tobacco Factory Theatres); *Banksy: The Room in the Elephant* (Tobacco Factory Theatres/Traverse Theatre); *Edward Gant's Amazing Feats of Loneliness, Wicked Lady* (Bristol Old Vic Theatre School), *The Picture of John Grey* (The Old Red Lion); *Measure for Measure* (Oxford School of Drama).

Opera includes: *Don Giovanni* (Hampstead Garden Opera), *A Midsummer Night's Dream* (The RSC & Garsington Opera).

Rajiv Pattani Lighting Designer

Rajiv is one of the Technicians at the Bush, working with Production Manager Michael and the creative teams to realise productions and events in both the Theatre and the Studio. He is also a lighting designer. Rajiv graduated from LAMDA in 2014 with qualifications in Stage Management and Technical Theatre, specialising in Lighting, Sound and AV. Recent design work for the Bush includes the reopening event *Black Lives, Black Words*, Edinburgh Fringe First winner 2017 *NASSIM* (Traverse 2/Bush Theatre/international tour), *Ramona Tells Jim* directed by Mel Hillyard and *Hijabi Monologues London*.

Other lighting design credits include: Network Theatre's *STUD* (Vault Festival 2018); *Screaming Secrets & Glass Roots* (Tristan Bates Theatre); Tom Stoppard's *On the Razzle* and Nina Raine's *Rabbit* (Pleasance Theatre for LAMDA productions); *Blood Wedding* (Bread & Roses Theatre); *Might Never Happen* (Doll's Eye Theatre Company); *Primadonna* (VAULT Festival 2016), as well as various projects at the Arcola, Hampstead and the Unicorn. Rajiv was also Production Electrician on *4 Minutes 12 Seconds* at Trafalgar Studios.

Ed Clarke Sound Designer
Ed has previously worked at the Bush Theatre on *The Royale*, *The Invisible*, *Perseverance Drive* and *Fear*. His other theatre credits include *All We Ever Wanted Was Everything* (Middle Child Theatre); *A Super Happy Story (About Feeling Super Sad)*, (Silent Uproar); *A Christmas Carol* and *A Short History of Tractors In Ukrainian* (Hull Truck Theatre); *Showboat* (New London Theatre); *The Infidel* (Theatre Royal Stratford East); *Orpheus* (Little Bulb Theatre at BAC and worldwide); *Baddies* (Unicorn Theatre); *The Realness, Politrix, Phoenix, KnifeEdge* and *Babylon* (The Big House); *Beauty and the Beast* (Young Vic and worldwide); Danny Boyle's *Frankenstein* (Olivier, National Theatre – Olivier Award nomination 2012); *Backbeat* (Duke of York's Theatre); *The Mysteries* and *The Good Hope* (National Theatre); *The Railway Children* (Waterloo International Station/Roundhouse Theatre Toronto); *Fatal Attraction* (Theatre Royal Haymarket); *Backbeat* (Duke of York's); *His Teeth* (Only Connect Theatre); *Baby Doll* (Albery Theatre); *Alex* (Arts Theatre, UK and international tour); *Old Times* and *A Doll's House* (Donmar Warehouse).

Thank Yous

Doreene Blackstock, Ben Bowles, Rachel Bown-Williams, Andy Bubble (Royal Exchange Theatre), Michael Buffong, Anastasia Chikezie, Ruth Cooper-Brown, Dr. Adam Elliott-Cooper, Simon Evans, Jessica Harwood (Watford Palace Theatre), Meg Hird, Hazel Holder (voice coach), Arinzé Kene, Erin Lee (National Theatre Archives), Lucie Pankhurst (movement director), Aleks Sierz, Roy Williams, Robert Witts (Coventry Archives) and CEG Hire & Productions

Bush Theatre

Bush
Theatre
We make theatre
for London. Now.

The Bush is a world-famous home for new plays
and an internationally renowned champion of
playwrights. We discover, nurture and produce
the best new writers from the widest range of
backgrounds from our home in a distinctive corner
of west London.

The Bush has won over 100 awards and developed
an enviable reputation for touring its acclaimed
productions nationally and internationally.

We are excited by exceptional new voices,
stories and perspectives – particularly those with
contemporary bite which reflect the vibrancy of
British culture now.

Located in the newly renovated old library on
Uxbridge Road in the heart of Shepherd's Bush,
the theatre houses two performance spaces, a
rehearsal room and the lively Library Bar.

Supported by
**ARTS COUNCIL
ENGLAND**

bushtheatre.co.uk

THANK YOU

The Bush Theatre would like to thank all its supporters whose valuable contributions have helped us to create a platform for our future and to promote the highest quality new writing, develop the next generation of creative talent and lead innovative community engagement work.

If you are interested in finding out how to be involved, please visit **bushtheatre.co.uk/support-us** or email **development@bushtheatre.co.uk** or call **020 8743 3584.**

Bush Theatre

PASSING THE BATON

Rediscovering the artists of colour who carved their way through British playwriting with distinction

Passing the Baton is a three-year initiative by the Bush Theatre to reacquaint theatre goers with playwrights who have been forgotten, are out of print and whose plays are not revived despite their status as critically acclaimed artists.

At the same time, a promising emerging writer of colour will be given a full length commission for the main house alongside mentoring to develop their work. In this way we will be passing the baton between established writers and emerging writers of colour.

In 2018 we introduce new audiences to *Leave Taking* by Winsome Pinnock, a playwright upon whose shoulders we now stand, and who paved the way for many of the writers and performers who appear at our home in Shepherd's Bush.

The first writer to receive the Passing the Baton commission is Kalungi Ssebandeke whose first full length play, *Assata Taught Me*, premiered at the Gate Theatre in 2017. He will receive mentoring by Winsome Pinnock and our literary team.

Leave Taking Production History

1987 Liverpool Playhouse
Opened 11 Nov 1987

Cast

Enid	Ellen Thomas
Del	Natasha Williams
Viv	Lisa Lewis
Mai	Lucita Lijertwood
Brod	Tommy Eytle

Creatives

Director	Kate Rowland
Designer	Boyes Candida
Lighting Designer	Les Lyon

1990 Lyric Hammersmith
26 July–25 August 1990
Opened 30 July 1990

Cast

Enid	Ellen Thomas
Del	Marianne Jean-Baptise
Viv	Pamela Nomvete
Mai	Corinne Skinner-Carter
Brod	Allister Bain

Creatives

Director	Hettie Macdonald
Designer	Catherine Armstrong
Lighting Designer	Tina MacHugh

1992 Belgrade Coventry
7–23 May 1992
Opened 11 May 1992

Cast

Enid	Anni Domingo
Del	Doreene Blackstock
Viv	Vivienne Rochester
Mai	Loren Rent
Brod	Eddie Osei

Creatives

Director	Rumu Sen-Gupta
Designer	Trudy Marklew
Lighting Designer	Alison Thorp
Sound Designer	Steve Wilson
Company Stage Manager	Cathryn Hatcher
Assistant Stage Manager	Nigel Mousley

1995 Cottesloe Theatre, National Theatre and NT Education UK tour
13 December 1994–12 April 1995
Opened 4 January 1995 Cottesloe Theatre

Cast

Enid	Jenni George
Del	Karen Tomlin
Viv	Ginny Holder
Mai	Doreen Ingleton
Brod	David Webber

Creatives

Director	Paulette Randall
Designer	Poppy Mitchell
Lighting Designer	Mark Ridler
Movement Director	'H' Patten
Sound Designer	Steven Brown

LEAVE TAKING

Winsome Pinnock

Introduction

I hadn't read *Leave Taking* for several years when Madani
Younis, Artistic Director of the Bush Theatre, told me that he
wanted to revive the play as part of the theatre's 2018 season.
He said that he and the Bush's creative team considered the play
a classic in the canon of work by black British playwrights and
that they felt that it remained relevant: Enid's predicament – the
plight of many immigrants regardless of where they come from,
caught between worlds – reaching out for life in a new country,
haunted by memories of what she has left behind.

On the first day of rehearsals at the Bush I was asked to talk to
the cast about how I came to write the play, the first full-length
play I had ever written. I found it difficult to answer the
question. Engaging with the text again had put me in
conversation with my younger self, who I felt was a presence in
the rehearsal room. I wished that she could answer for me.

I developed a passion for theatre and performance as a child of
around twelve years old when, with generous grants from the
GLC (Greater London Council), our school took us on visits to
the theatre. I wouldn't have gone otherwise. There wasn't
enough money in our household to afford such trips and there
wasn't enough time either. The interest was awoken, and, along
with my younger sister, I became part of a group of young
people who became regular theatregoers. We were given the
resources (by our school, youth theatres and drama clubs) to
dance, act and write. My mother offered quiet encouragement.
When I doubted myself, she reminded me that success was
usually a matter of holding on, of seeing things through to the
end. When I expressed a desire to play the piano I came home
from school one day to discover that she had purchased a piano
so old it had a few missing keys, but it was functional. She
found me a teacher: Miss Wright who lived off the Holloway
Road and taught local kids to play at 15p a lesson. My mother

and siblings listened tirelessly to the stories I wrote as a child; I was the acknowledged writer of the family.

My mother migrated from Jamaica to the United Kingdom in 1959, following her husband-to-be who, like Enid's spouse in *Leave Taking*, saved his salary for a whole year before he was able to afford the money to buy a ticket for her passage over. The shock and disappointment of those who migrated to the UK at that time is well documented. My parents' generation had been indoctrinated by a colonialist education that lionised all things British. They celebrated Empire Day (24th May) when their schools distributed British flags and lollipops. Despite their disappointment on entering a country whose environment was often hostile ('No blacks, no dogs, no Irish!'), they didn't complain and rarely discussed the hardships. After all, they had grown up on plantation villages where the legacy of enslavement was still evident in the wretched poverty they endured. Jamaica achieved independence the year that my youngest sibling was born. My parents' marriage disintegrated a few years later, and my mother became a single parent to four young children at a time when there was still stigma attached to divorce.

Writers are given their preoccupations at birth. I am the descendant of enslaved Africans who were forcibly denied the right to the written word, or to express themselves through art or song and yet held on to aspects of their African heritage in both. Traces of African spiritual rituals were preserved by clandestine practices like obeah, which was made illegal in Jamaica in 1898, a law that remains on the statute books. Despite its illegality, my mother and some of her peers retained an interest in obeah, consulting obeah men and women in times of crisis for advice and healing.

As a schoolgirl I thought I was going to be an actress. I idolised Glenda Jackson and longed to follow in her footsteps. When I left school, the headmistress predicted that I had a future in the industry. At university I was told that, although I was considered a talented actress, I probably wouldn't be cast in many productions because I was black. I focused on my writing. I had started writing a play (a sketch really) about two

girls getting ready to go out but never managing to leave their
bedroom. I sent it to the Royal Court Young Writers' Group and
was invited to join. It was there that I wrote *Leave Taking*, my
first full-length play, when I was twenty-three years old. I
wanted to make Enid the heroine of the play because I couldn't
recall ever seeing such a character – a hospital cleaner – as the
lead in a British play. I specifically wanted to write about the
black British experience as distinct from African American
culture because producers often seemed to think that they are
interchangeable. I submitted the play to the Royal Court's
literary department who sent me an encouraging rejection letter.

I knuckled down to write another play – *A Hero's Welcome* –
which received a rehearsed reading at the Royal Court. As a
result of the reading I was commissioned by the Liverpool
Playhouse Studio and dusted off *Leave Taking*, restructuring
and rewriting to their financial requirements – the budget would
only allow for five characters and two sets, so I cut characters
and locations. This meant that I could focus more on Enid's
relationship with her daughters, Del and Viv. I was a young
feminist. At consciousness-raising groups the mantra 'the
personal is political' was drummed into me. Similarly, at the
Royal Court Young Writers' Group we were encouraged by
workshop leaders Hanif Kureishi and Stephen Wakelam to
'write what you know'. I now understand that you write what
you come to know. Writing is an exploration, the pursuit of the
answer to an unanswerable question. I started out wanting to
write about the daughters – this new breed of black British
woman – but ended up fascinated by Enid and the complexity
of her relationship with England, her daughters, and herself, as
well as her long-standing friendship with Brod whom she has
known since childhood. Brod and Enid have travelled a great
distance, both physically and psychologically. They would not
have survived without each other. Mai is an enigmatic figure,
especially for Viv and Del who have no direct connection with
the culture she represents, but she comes to have a powerful
influence on all of them.

Leave Taking has been produced four times (the 2018 Bush
production will be its fifth production) since 1987. Years after

the play was produced at the National Theatre (1994) I was told that it was the first play written by a black British woman to have been produced there. I also learned that it was the first time that a black woman writer and director (Paulette Randall) had worked together at the venue. After the first performances of the play at the Liverpool Playhouse Studio women from different cultural backgrounds collared me to say: 'That's my story. I'm Enid' or 'That's my mam. She's just like Enid.'

The young woman who wrote *Leave Taking* had no idea that a generation who were very young children or who hadn't been born when it was first produced would feel that the play still speaks to their experience. I hope it will connect with new audiences in the same way. Some of the speeches feel as though they were written recently: Brod's words about having to seek naturalisation after thinking of himself as a British citizen for his whole life echo words spoken thirty years later by victims of the 2018 Windrush scandal (a misnomer considering it involves immigrants from diverse backgrounds and not just the Caribbean).

When I was a child my mother told me that she thought that I might have a gift for clairvoyance. I understand now that she had always instinctively known that I was a writer. It's not that writers are necromancers, but when I read the play I raise again the spirits of those characters. I hear their voices very clearly; I see my younger self consulting with my mother, asking her how you make chocolate tea, and hear her ribbing me all over again about the royalties I owe her or joking that I should credit her as co-writer. I experience again the writing of the scene where Enid breaks down. I know what that feels like now because I have lived through it. I want to ask that young woman if, when she wrote the play, she would ever have imagined that she too would one day howl with grief into a rainy London night after witnessing her mother take her last breath just as Enid howls for a mother she will never hold again.

Winsome Pinnock
London, 2018

Leave Taking was first performed at the Liverpool Playhouse Studio, on 11 November 1987. The cast was as follows:

ENID MATTHEWS	Ellen Thomas
DEL MATTHEWS	Natasha Williams
VIV MATTHEWS	Lisa Lewis
MAI	Lucita Lijertwood
BRODERICK	Tommy Eytle

Director	Kate Rowland
Designer	Candida Boyes
Lighting	Les Lyon

*For Nada Pinnock-Graham (1929–2015),
with love and immense gratitude*

'These grandmothers and mothers of ours [were] driven to a numb and bleeding madness by the springs of creativity in them for which there was no release… Throwing away this spirituality was their pathetic attempt to lighten the soul to a weight their work-worn, sexually abused bodies could bear.'

Alice Walker, In Search of Our Mothers' Gardens

'[A mother accepts] a daughter with the bitter pleasure of self-recognition in another victim, and at the same time feels guilty for having brought her into the world.'

Simone de Beauvoir, The Second Sex

Characters

MAI, *an obeah woman*
ENID MATTHEWS, *forties*
DEL MATTHEWS, *Enid's daughter, eighteen*
VIV MATTHEWS, *Enid's daughter, seventeen*
BRODERICK, *a family friend, late forties/fifties*

Scene One

MAI's bedsit. Very messy. The table centre stage is covered in papers, playing cards scattered all over, a glass of water and the remains of a half-burnt white candle. At the table, two chairs. MAI sits in the armchair. She wears a cardigan over her dress. She's slumped in the armchair, drinking from a bottle of stout. On her lap is a book which she picks up, finds her page and tries to read, having to hold it away from her and close her eyes tight. She picks up a pen and starts to write a note on the book, then throws her pen down.

MAI. Lord, see my troubles now.

> *She curls and uncurls her fingers and bends her arm at the elbow, then stops to pick the pen up again. There is a knock at the door. This startles MAI who sits up abruptly and gives a soft belch. Knocking continues. MAI quietly puts down the stout bottle, hoping they will go away, but the knocking is persistent.*

> What the hell… (*Calls, polite.*) Who is it?

ENID. Enid Matthews.

MAI (*puzzled, to herself*). Enid Matthews? (*Calls.*) What you want?

ENID. I have a appointment.

MAI. We closed. Come back on Thursday.

ENID. After I come from so far?

MAI. Is Bank Holiday…

ENID. Please. I pay five pound more.

> MAI *thinks for a moment.*

MAI. The Good Lord did say that money isn't everything. But when duty call, it call.

MAI opens the door. ENID *comes in followed by her daughters* VIV *and* DEL.

I sometimes regret the day Mother discovered I had the gift. Since I was thirteen I ain't had a moment's peace.

ENID. I did ring make appointment. You remember?

MAI. You must be speak to me secretary.

ENID. I bring me daughters with me.

MAI. Some people don't like that, but I don't mind it. I have a son meself, but him lef' home long time.

ENID. Them tell me say you have the gift good.

MAI. These days people does just want me to help them win on the Mirror Bingo. Them nuh know say me nah work with numbers. I don't deal in numbers. Is people I deal in. (*To* GIRLS.) Unno ever read before?

No reply from DEL *and* VIV.

Unno scared a me? Is so young people does scared a obeah woman. Can't keep any secret from Mai. Mai see right through to your soul. (*To* ENID.) That would be ten pound
· extra on top a the special Bank Holiday price.

ENID. Long as we get a reading.

MAI. Sit down m'dear. Must be tired come all this way.

They do so.

Unno want a cup a tea?

The GIRLS *open their mouths to speak but* ENID *is there first.*

ENID. We all right, thank you.

MAI. Eager for you reading, ennit? Plenty a time fe that m'dear. I like to get to know me client first. Have a cup a tea, a biscuit, a chat. You relax, I relax, see.

ENID. We don't have much time. Not many bus running today.

MAI. You definitely need a hot drink after waiting out in the cold.

ENID. All right.

MAI. Let me put the kettle on. (*Picks up stout bottle as she goes. Apologetic.*) Bank Holiday.

She's gone.

DEL. She stinks.

ENID. Shush.

VIV. It's incense.

DEL. End up paying fifty quid time she's finished with you.

VIV. Frankincense and myrrh.

ENID. That any a your business?

DEL. Mumbo-jumbo nonsense.

VIV. I'm hungry.

DEL. Maybe our hostess'll rustle you up a little something. If you pay her enough.

ENID. Don't eat anything she give you. We not here for dinner.

VIV. She's not going to read me on me own is she?

ENID. I want to hear what she got to say.

DEL. Thought a reading was supposed to be private.

ENID. As long as I'm the one paying…

DEL. Don't even want one.

ENID. Then why you come?

DEL. I didn't realise I had a choice.

VIV. Look at this.

DEL. Don't touch the woman's things.

VIV. It's like a museum.

DEL. Don't know why you didn't just carry us to the doctor's.

VIV. Shut up, Del.

DEL. It's true. I know what she's after.

VIV. Can she really read the future? She tell me what grades I'll get in the exams?

ENID. You see how she stay? Don't push me, Del.

VIV. Can she Mum?

ENID. 'Member when Miss Pannycook have that car accident? A she predict that.

VIV. Spooky dooky.

DEL. Predicted it or caused it? (*Stands and looks around the room*.) What a mess. I bet there's rats.

VIV. It's not dirty, though.

ENID. When she bring the tea just pretend you drinking it, then let it go cold.

DEL (*holding a glass from the table up to the light*). Reckon she does what you do and nicks holy water off the Roman Catholics?

ENID. You want people hear you?

VIV. No one's listening, Mum.

DEL. Fancy nicking holy water to practise voodoo.

ENID. You go too far, Delores.

VIV. It's not voodoo.

DEL. Obeah.

VIV. Sit down, Del. You're making me nervous.

ENID. I might get a bath if she don't charge too much extra.

VIV. You had a bath this morning.

DEL. A holy bath, stupid. Stinks.

ENID. The older you get, the more you find out you got to
    protect yourself.

VIV. From what?

ENID. You will learn.

DEL (*teasing* VIV). Evil spirits… Duppies and rolling calves.

    MAI *puts her head round the door.*

MAI. Lady, you can help me with the tray, please?

ENID. You two sit still and behave.

    MAI *and* ENID *go to the kitchen.*

DEL. 'You two sit still and behave.' She thinks we're seven
    years old.

VIV. Why do you always have to argue with her? Why can't
    you just pretend to do what she says?

DEL. Anything for a quiet life, eh Viv?

VIV. Both as bad as each other.

MAI. Look lady, if is man you come 'bout you might as well go
    straight home. Plenty black woman over here does come see
    me 'bout man: how to catch him, how to get rid of him, how
    to get him back. Mostly them does want to get him back. So
    many a those women lef' lonely on them own. Some a them
    gone mad over man. They think I can work miracles.

ENID. Me husban' long gone, yes. But I don't want him back. I
    bring up those two girls on me own.

MAI. So what you want me to do for you?

ENID. I want a reading. And maybe a healing bath.

DEL. Stop staring at me.

MAI. I don't do bath any more. Landlady complain say me a
    bring stranger inna she house use bath. Think she going
    catch something. How she going catch anything when all my
    clients much cleaner than she?

ENID (*reaching inside her bag, takes out a letter*). A month ago
  me sister send me this letter say me mother sick, need money
  for doctor. The woman so lie. I don't know whether to
  believe her or not. How I know she nah want the money for
  herself? You could give me some guidance?

MAI. Cost you extra....

  ENID *nods and hands* MAI *a letter.* MAI *holds the letter
  away from her then puts on her glasses (which hang around
  her neck). She reads.*

VIV. Still feel ill?

DEL. I'm all right now.

VIV. You should see a doctor.

DEL. I'm fine.

VIV. Might be something serious.

DEL. It's not. All right?

VIV. Some girl in school kept getting these stomach pains...

DEL. Shut up.

VIV. Shall I open a window?

DEL. It's supposed to stink. Part of the atmosphere, ennit?

VIV. I like it.

DEL. You would.

VIV. Did you know there's as many obeah women in the West
  Indies as priests?

DEL. How d'you know that? Read it in a book?

VIV. Uncle Brod said.

DEL. Oh yeah?

VIV. He should know. He was born there.

MAI. You send money home?

ENID. I do my best, but every week me sister send another letter a beg me for this and a beg me for that. Is not as if I don't write tell her how things hard over here. She must think I'm living like a millionaire.

MAI. When last you go back there?

ENID. Five years ago.

MAI. And you mother?

ENID. If the woman didn't climb tree, pick coconut give me.

MAI. Five years is a long time.

ENID. Woman strong as she don't suffer from disease like that.

MAI. Them bring doctor to her?

ENID. So them say. But like I tell you, me sister so lie you don't know if is true. How I know she not going to spend the money on herself like last time? Mother on dying. (*Kisses her teeth.*) Me gran'mother live till she a hundred and two.

VIV (*picks up an African figure*). Look at this.

MAI *folds the letter hands it back to* ENID.

DEL. What is it?

VIV. There's writing on the bottom, see?

DEL *reads then drops it.*

DEL. Fucking stupid.

VIV. What's it say? (*Picks it up and reads, laughs.*) You believe that? (*Waves figurine around.*)

DEL. Course not. Get off me.

ENID. You can tell me if is sick she really sick?

MAI. M'dear, that not the way the spirit work.

VIV. Wouldn't it be funny if she really did have powers?

ENID. You a obeah woman and you can't tell me if a lie she a tell?

DEL. No chance.

MAI. Send them what them ask for. You mother could do with it anyway.

VIV (*puts figure back*). I want to go to the West Indies. It's not all white sandy beaches, you know. Uncle Brod says you don't know who you are 'less you've been there. (*Finds MAI's book stuffed in the sofa and pulls it out.*)

DEL. I already know who I am.

ENID. Do the older girl first. She badly in need of a reading.

MAI. A woman compel her daughter into a reading is usually something she want to know about the girl. What you want to know, Enid Matthews?

ENID. She getting outta hand. She don't come home after work.

VIV (*reading the spine of the book*). 'Charms and Counter Charms, Divination and Demonology'.

MAI. So, she go out with she friends. Nothing wrong with that.

ENID. Sometime she don't come home till the early hours. An' is me one sitting up worrying.

DEL (*opens a box on the table, takes out lucky charms*). Look at these.

MAI. You should go to bed. People does take advantage if you show them you care so much. Take my advice: leave her to do what she want and get yourself a good night sleep. That's what I would do.

ENID. I shoulda had boys.

MAI. Yes. Boys can fight, throw licks, and petrol bombs.

ENID. She never used to be like this. All on a sudden she change, won't listen to me any more. Angry. Like she possessed. Nah mus' something make her change so?

MAI. You think is evil spirit?

ENID. What else?

VIV (*reading*). Bloody hell.

MAI. An' who you think set that spirit on you?

ENID. Thas why I come here. For you to help me. Please read the big one first.

DEL (*rummaging through the lucky charms*). You should take one of these in the exam with you for good luck.

A cock crows.

What's that?

VIV *dashes to the window and looks out.*

VIV. Chickens!

DEL. You're joking.

VIV. Come and have a look.

DEL *goes to the window.*

Look at the little fat one.

DEL. Fucking farmyard.

VIV. Randy little thing's trying to get his leg over. She doesn't wanna know.

DEL. Don't blame her. Look at the stomach on it. Go on, girl. Peck his eyes out.

ENID *and* MAI *come in holding teacups.*

MAI. I think that one mad, you know. He sleep all day and crow at midnight.

VIV. You allowed to keep chickens in Deptford?

MAI. Why not? Is a free country, ennit? I couldn't live without a few fowl in the backyard.

VIV. Do you use them for… your work?

MAI. That was the old-time obeah. I keep them as pets. (*To* VIV.) We leave you tea in the kitchen. Wait in there till we finish with you sister.

ENID. Go on.

VIV *goes out.*

ENID *moves to the back of the room.* MAI *goes to the door.*

MAI. Come sit, nuh.

DEL *sits.*

DEL. This is stupid.

MAI. You don't like read? (*Putting* DEL *at ease.*) They all like that at first, but by the end I have to force them out the door. And they always come back. What you want? Palm or card?

ENID. Palm.

MAI *takes* DEL*'s palm, looks at it then looks into* DEL*'s eyes, then down at her palm again. She passes her hand over* DEL*'s palm, then looks into it again.* DEL *giggles.* MAI *closes her eyes, head up as if muttering some prayer.* DEL *drags her hand away.*

DEL. I've had enough of this.

ENID. Sit down, Del.

DEL. Read palms, Jesus!

MAI. Calm down, girl. I won't hurt you.

DEL. You won't get the chance. You're not gonna see anything in my palm. It's in here you wanna look at. She wants to know if I'm pregnant.

MAI. Then she come to the wrong place.

ENID. Who tell you that? You see how she stay?

MAI. Please, not so loud… The landlady.

DEL. She's obsessed. I see you watching my stomach, making what you think are discreet enquiries about my periods. Wouldn't surprise me if she kept a diary.

MAI (*to* ENID). I'm not a doctor.

DEL. Can't have a bath without her poking her nose through the keyhole.

ENID. Shame me in front a people.

MAI. I can only predict and protect.

ENID. I asking you to protect my daughter.

MAI. They have these clinics…

ENID. And me a go pay you good money…

DEL. Wasting money you ain't got on this rubbish.

> VIV *enters*.

VIV. When's it my turn?

ENID. How much I owe you?

MAI. I din do nuttin.

ENID (*takes money out of her purse and puts it on the table*). For you time. (*To* VIV.) Come, let's go.

VIV. But I haven't had a reading yet.

ENID. Let's go.

> ENID *and* VIV *go*. DEL *hangs back*.

MAI. Kiss me beak. (*Slight pause*.) What a bank holiday.

DEL. Waste of time.

> DEL *starts to go*.

MAI. Anytime you need someone to talk to, I'm always here.

DEL. Don't believe in that mumbo-jumbo shit.

MAI. I can see you need to talk.

DEL. How? Read me mind? I got friends I wanna talk.

MAI. Yes?

DEL. I'm going.

MAI. All right.

DEL. You might fool the old lady, but you can't fool me. I know your game.

MAI. You do?

DEL. Duppies and evil spirits. Give us a break.

    DEL *starts to go*.

MAI. And I know your game… (*Holds her hand out*.) The charm, please.

    DEL *stops*.

DEL. What you on about?

MAI. Read my mind.

    DEL *contemplates a stand-off but* MAI *doesn't back down, so she reluctantly digs into her pocket and retrieves the charm, which she places on* MAI'*s open palm.* DEL *leaves*.

Scene Two

A few days later.

ENID'*s living room. Evening.* ENID *wears her work overalls and is cleaning up, scrubbing at the floor while* VIV, *wearing a dress, sits on the sofa, books balanced on her lap, making notes.*

VIV. I wish you'd let me help you.

ENID. You get on with your work.

    VIV *watches* ENID *scrubbing at the carpet.*

VIV. Out, out damned spot.

ENID. Eh?

VIV. Shakespeare.

ENID (*enjoying saying it*). Shakespeare.

VIV (*posher*). Shakespeare.

ENID (*mimicking*). Shakespeare.

>   ENID *resumes her scrubbing.*

>   Out out, damn spot.

VIV. It's not a magic spell, Mum.

>   *They share a smile before each resumes her work.*

ENID. How come I never hear Del come in last night?

VIV. She didn't want to wake you up.

ENID. And you say she leave out to work early this morning?

VIV. That's right.

ENID. Leave out to work in the burger place?

VIV. Ah-hah.

ENID. You did tell her 'bout Pastor an' him wife?

VIV. She said she'd be back before they get here.

ENID. Pastor say all the family have to be here when him do
the blessing.

>   *Pause.*

>   You sure she come home last night?

VIV. Don't you believe me?

ENID. I was just wondering how she go to work in a place that
give her the sack two week ago.

VIV. Oh...

ENID. Oh-oh.

VIV. Promise me you're not going to make a scene.

>   ENID *continues scrubbing.*

>   Please, Mum.

>   BRODERICK *enters wearing an old suit. His tie hangs
>   around his neck.*

BROD. Do this for me nuh, Enid?

ENID. You can't do it yourself?

BROD. I'm not used to wearing tie. Feel like the devil a
strangle me.

VIV. That'll be the evil spirit, Uncle Brod.

BROD. Carpet nuh clean yet?

ENID. This is a map a your life, Brod: wine stain, Guinness,
brandy...

BROD. Poor man not suppose to be sober, Enid. Last time I
sober me think me dead an' gone a hell. (*Beat.*) You think I
should give Pastor a sniff a that white rum I been keeping
warm under me mattress since Christmas?

ENID (*warning*). Brod.

BROD. How else we going entertain the man?

ENID. Talk to him.

BROD. Boy, I can see we in for a hell of a evening.

ENID *stops scrubbing, takes off her rubber gloves.*

ENID. What you think?

BROD. This is the cleanest flat on the estate. Place don't need
no blessing, Enid. The smell a bleach frighten off every
duppy from here to the Elephant and Castle. (*Picks up*
ENID*'s list, reads.*) 'Clean carpet. Wine glasses, set oven for
chicken. Make sure Brod have tie.' Boy, we really turn
English now. What she did know about list before she come
here? Back home we keep everything in we head.

ENID (*takes the list and stuffs it in her pocket*). And don't it
show, Brod? (*Fixes* BROD*'s tie.*)

BROD. When you mother was the same age as you, the amount
a things she had to do before the sun even rise. And she
never need no list to do it neither.

ENID. Keep you skin quiet, Brod. I got enough to be doing
without you taking yourself make joke.

BROD (*pinching* VIV *to let her in on the joke*). Miss Enid oh, you can't find a different pair a shoes? With them shoes I can see right through to you crack foot-bottom.

ENID (*quickly*). Where?

BROD *and* VIV *laugh*.

Think you funny, ennit, Brod? One day God going give you joke, but you won't be the one laughing. I will.

BROD (*to* VIV, *still teasing* ENID). You never wonder why you mother foot-bottom crack so?

ENID. Shut up you mouth, man.

BROD. Back home she used to rise with the dawn, and she was on them feet, bare feet, all day: climb high hill, walk over big stone to fetch water from gully, work in the field pick coffee, plantain, then sell it a market.

ENID. Brod, what the use you telling her these things? She don't understand that way a life.

BROD. Well, she should. (*To* VIV.) You mother don't like to talk 'bout back home. Me, I dream about the land a wood and water. Pure rainforest.

ENID. Then why you nuh go back there you have such a longing for it? I don't dream about back home because this is my home.

BROD. A few years ago, I woulda say the same thing. All my life I think of meself as a British subject, wave a flag on Empire Day, touch me hat whenever me see a picture a the queen. Then them send me letter say if me don't get me nationality paper in order they going kick me outta the country. You mother, same thing. Ennit, Enid?

VIV. Kick us out? Where would me and Del go?

BROD. Call me a alien. As if me live the last thirty years on the moon instead of on this blasted estate. I had to pay fifty pounds to become a citizen. After me spend the whole a me life standing to attention whenever me hear the national anthem.

ENID. So, we pay the fifty pound and now we nationality
    secure.

BROD. Secure what? Till them change them mind again? 'This
    is my home.' (*Kisses his teeth*.) I make sure me Jamaican
    passport up to date. An' you better do the same.

ENID. You read Viv school report?

VIV. Mum.

ENID. All 'A's. My daughter going to university. How many a
    my sister children back home going to university?

BROD. And you know why they ain't going to university?
    Because they too poor. An' why they poor? Because a
    colonialism. Imperialism. Vampirism. They suck the blood
    outta the island, suck them dry.

ENID. If me sister and her husband did get up off them
    backside and work that piece a land then maybe they come
    to something.

BROD. That dry piece a land can't grow nuttin, Miss Enid.

ENID. Them fall down a imperialism. Them catch cold a
    imperialism. When unno going to take responsibility? Me,
    I don't rely on nobody but meself.

BROD. You remember Gullyman, Enid?

ENID. Long time now me nuh see Gullyman.

BROD. Man mad walk street no shoes, no socks, shirt open
    down to him navel. In the cold. Man a walk an' shake. Beg
    me fifty pence for a cup a tea. Didn't even recognise me.

ENID. You see where me put me Bible?

BROD (*to* VIV). Gullyman come over here with two dollar in
    him pocket. But Gullyman could work, and he had a talent
    for saving. Within three years Gullyman buy car – old car
    granted, but car all the same – an' house. Gullyman forget
    everybody – all him friends, him people back home, just cut
    everybody off. You meet him in the road, him wouldn't see
    you. Too high. Remember how him use to talk, Enid?

ENID. Like him have cork in him nose hole.

BROD. An' he was always correcting people. 'Don't say wartar, man. Say wortur.' One mornin Gullyman wake up to find him lovely car covered in shit an a message on him door read 'wogs out'. Gullyman heart brock, him mind crack, and now he can hardly talk broken English.

VIV. That's sad, man.

BROD. English.

ENID. You come here, you try to fit in. Stick to the rules. England been good to me. I proud a my English girls.

BROD. You teaching these children all wrong. They going forget where them come from. These girls ain't English like them newsreader who got English stamp on them like the letters on a stick a rock, right through English. These girls got Caribbean souls.

VIV. Don't you mean African souls?

ENID. Don't talk foolish. African...

BROD. Girl, you a 'A'-class student... Tell me what you know about Nanny a the Maroons.

VIV. Never heard of her.

ENID. Stop with you stupidness Brod.

BROD. Jamaica, 1730... something: The maroons – slaves descended from the Ashanti warrior tribes – escape from captivity and run away to the Blue Mountains. Nanny, an Ashanti warrior queen, a powerful obeah woman, becomes their leader. When the English fire musket, them bullet bounce off Nanny shoulders kill the men who was trying to destroy her. A she lead the slave rebellions. You, my dear, are descended from Queen Nanny.

VIV. Am I?

BROD. Is in the blood. Thas why black woman so strong. Look at your mother.

ENID. Viv, you intelligent. You mustn't encourage him.

BROD. You mix these children up, Enid.

ENID. Mix up what? They know who they are. She know who she is. Tell him who you are.

VIV (*stands, recites*).
'A dust whom England bore, shaped, made aware…
A body of England's, breathing English air,
Washed by the rivers, blest by the suns of home.'

ENID (*not quite sure how to take this*). You see… see. 'Breathing English air'… English.

ENID *goes*.

BROD (*shouts through the door at* ENID). So, why you have her lock up with book all day long? If she is a – (*Mock accent.*) Hinglish girl like how you say she is she should be out with her boyfriend every single night like all the other Hinglish girls.

VIV (*laughing*). I haven't got a boyfriend.

BROD. Keep a lookout for me.

VIV. What?

BROD. The door.

VIV. What you up to, Uncle Brod?

BROD (*taking a hip flask from his pocket*). We going to need a little Jamaican courage if we going to get through this evening in one piece.

BROD *hands flask to* VIV, *who takes a swig*.

VIV. She means well you know.

BROD. You telling me? I know you mother long before you was born.

VIV. She works so hard. I don't know how she does it.

BROD. She do it for you.

VIV. How can I ever live up to that? We don't deserve it, Brod.

BROD. She think you deserve it. Make her happy and accept that.

VIV. What did she want? When she was my age, what did she want?

BROD. You mother did want turn postmistress, but she never pass the exam. She want better for you.

VIV. And what if I fail my exams? What'll she do then?

BROD. Trust me, you won't fail, not if Enid have anything to do with it.

   VIV *returns to her books*. BROD *removes the record, takes up another record, reads the label, puts it on the record player, it is heavy dub*. BROD *nods his head like a man tasting something he doesn't expect to like and discovering that it's actually quite nice*.

VIV. What sort of shit did they cover Gullyman's car with? Dog or human?

BROD. Bullshit, dogshit… Shit is shit, Viv. A racist is a man who stick him fist inna him own backside then tell everybody else how them hand stink.

   ENID *returns*. ENID *has taken off her overalls and headscarf to reveal her Sunday best*.

But stop. What is this vision of beauty? Queen Nanny come down from the Blue Mountains.

VIV. You look really nice, Mum.

ENID. You think so?

BROD. You going keep the hat on?

ENID. You don't like it?

BROD. English people don't wear hat inside the house.

   ENID *removes the hat*.

ENID. Better?

BROD. This pastor must be a very high man. You sure you not in love with him?

ENID. Him have a wife.

BROD. That don't bother some man.

ENID (*pointed*). No, it doesn't bother some man, does it, Brod? (*Removes the record and replaces it with the hymns.*)

VIV. What you two talking about?

BROD (*to* ENID). Nuttin.

VIV (*rolling her eyes*). You lot never tell me anything.

The sound of the front door.

BROD. You want me and Viv to go in the kitchen?

ENID. Stay you bound, Brod.

VIV. Remember, you're not going to make a scene.

DEL *enters to silence. She's wearing her work uniform.*

DEL. What's up? This place looks like a funeral parlour.

ENID. Viv never tell you about Pastor?

DEL. Yeah, she told me… yeah.

ENID. Where you been, Del?

VIV. Mum, I told you…

ENID *holds up her hand.*

ENID. I want you to tell me.

DEL *looks to* VIV *who is unable to rescue her.*

DEL. We had a busy day and they asked me to work late and I needed the overtime so…

ENID. You never come home last night.

DEL. Why don't you believe anything I say?

ENID. I did ring them up. Them say you never go in.

DEL. I was too sick to go in. See, last night I slept on
someone's floor and caught a chill.

ENID. Don't lie to me, girl. You didn't go in because you have
a argument with the manager and they tell you not to come
back.

Slight pause.

DEL. He talks to me as if I can't speak English.

ENID. You think it easy to find a job these days?

DEL. I'll sign on tomorrow.

ENID. You will look for another job tomorrow.

DEL. All right, Mummy. Anything you say.

ENID. Don't laugh at me, girl.

DEL. You can't talk to me like that. I'm not some kid.

ENID. Long as you living under my roof you will work. I don't
want people saying we lazy.

DEL. All right.

ENID. Now go and take off those clothes and come back down
and wait for Pastor.

Pause.

DEL. All I did last night was dance. What's wrong with that? I
like dancing. I been following that sound system for years.
The bass is mad. You wanna see it pounding the walls, like
one big pulsing heart. When that bass gets inside you and
flings you round the room you can't do nothing to stop it.

BROD. Sound like you was in the spirit.

ENID. I don't want to hear this. Go and get changed.

Slight pause. DEL *doesn't move.*

DEL. I hate it here.

ENID. You ungrateful…

BROD. Let it rest. We not going to get anywhere by fighting each other.

DEL. Grateful for what? This shithole? A greasy job in a greasy café where they treat me like a dum dum and give me a couple of pounds at the end of every week? What's that to be grateful for?

ENID. I work two jobs seven days a week to put food in you belly and roof over you head. I wear one dress, one pair a shoes with hole in it so that you can dress like those children who have fathers. People laugh at me, but they never laugh at you.

DEL. But what you give us that we can use out there? You don't see the police vans hunting us down, or the managers who treat us like we're the lowest of the low. You're too busy bowing and scraping to your beloved England. And where's it got you? Remember her works do at the hospital last Christmas?

VIV. Stop it, Del.

ENID. Let her talk. I'm listening.

DEL. You're all dressed up and you look beautiful. We're having fun. Then one of the nurses drinks too much and pukes all over the floor, remember that? And, in front of everyone, matron tells you to clean it up. You put your overalls on over your beautiful dress; in front of everyone there, you get a mop and bucket and clean it up. Yes, England loves you, all right. No wonder Dad left you.

ENID *slaps* DEL.

Pause. For a moment it looks as though DEL *might hit her back.*

DEL. That's the last time.

DEL *leaves.*

VIV *goes after her.*

ENID. People grow up in England think they can talk to you anyhow. Well, they can't.

BROD. Pastor soon come.

ENID. Yes, we better get the wine out the fridge.

BROD. You all right, Miss Enid?

ENID. Yes, yes Brod. Just leave me.

ENID *and* BROD *continue to prepare for the Pastor's visit as the scene ends.*

Scene Three

A few hours later. Late evening. ENID *is tidying up.* BROD *sits on the sofa, loosening his tie.* ENID *hums 'Nothing but the Blood of Jesus' as she clears up.* BROD *takes a surreptitious swig from his flask then tucks into the leftover nibbles, contributing the odd line to the hymn.*

ENID. Well, thank God we get through it.

BROD. I was all right?

ENID. You did look sharp, Brod man. What I would do without you?

BROD. The hard part was to drink in little sips. Pastor does always take little sip like that?

ENID. He's a high man. It look bad that Viv and Del wasn't here?

BROD. Pastor have him head too far up him hole to notice.

ENID. Place just bless an' you talking dirty?

BROD. Sorry, Miss Enid. You right.

ENID. Why them have to be so rude?

BROD. Rude? You seen them kids rioting on TV? Thas what you call rude.

ENID. You always take them side. I'm always the one in the wrong, ennit?

BROD. You really think them a go entertain you guest after the fight unno did have?

ENID. I feel so shame when Pastor ask me where them was. You think him know me was lying?

BROD. Pastor Trent have many quality, but I don't believe he have the gift a sight.

ENID. When I need my daughters' support they running wild.

BROD. Those girls ain't wild, Enid.

ENID. You nuh have a hard word to say about anything. Long as you have your glass a whisky or white rum, everything roses.

BROD. I can be tough when I need to be.

ENID. At least it wasn't a disaster.

BROD. Why you so bothered about what these people think?

ENID. Where would I bring my problems if I din't have the church? Who listen to me apart from God?

BROD. Obeah woman?

ENID. Me finish with obeah woman.

BROD. Why? She nuh good? Remember that accident with Sister Pannycook? / A she predict that.

ENID. A she predict that. I know, but I have made a covenant with God.

BROD. I just don't understand the church business these days. The spirit gone outta it. All that talk about saving souls. What special occasion they saving them for? Is all pay now and enjoy later.

ENID (*smiling*). You too bad, Brod.

BROD. Pastor put me in mind a Gullyman. You notice the resemblance? All the time he talking him wringing him hand and walking backward. Him an' him wife jus' want an easy life, discuss Bible over tea in china cup. In my day it was about throwing yourself right on the edge of life. It was jumping and shouting and feeling the damn thing, feeling the spirit flame up inside you.

ENID. That why you does drink so much rum these days? To feel the fire flaming up inside you again?

BROD. Don't make fun, Enid. I drink my drink and dreams does come to me.

ENID. Spen' half you life flat-out drunk.

BROD. Not drunk, Enid. In the spirit.

ENID. You in the spirit all right.

BROD. I can see things that Pastor could only dream of. Visions. Bible reading. The man too speaky spoky. See him an' him wife a look round 'It good enough? These people good enough?' That man don't know how to tie down demons. Back home the church was hot. Pastor Chully Johnson... Now, that was a man could wrestle with demon. 'Member that night Hurricane Hanley blow through May Pen? Chully Johnson hold a service to tie it down. Jesus Christ. Hanley rip through the houses, tear up trees, throw them high in a the sky but Johnson nuh 'fraid a hurricane. Him shout out 'Stand firm my brothers and sisters. Satan will not take possession of this meeting house tonight. I rebuke you, Satan!' Boy, that night Chully call down a spirit more powerful than any hurricane.

ENID. That service was sweet.

BROD. Spirit fling Mooma round the room till she burst out talking in tongues, remember?

ENID. We was all talking in tongues that night, Brod.

BROD *imitates talking in tongues*.

Quiet nuh, man. Yuh want the neighbours to hear you?

BROD *continues to talk in tongues. Despite herself,* ENID *laughs.*

BROD. Good to see you laughing. You in a party mood? Listen to this.

BROD *puts a record on. It is heavy dub. He closes his eyes and feels the music.* ENID *taps her feet.* BROD *opens his eyes. He takes her hands and pulls her up. They both feel the heavy bass moving through them, dancing together at first then separately in their own worlds.* VIV *enters and watches them. As the music comes to an end* VIV *goes back outside.* BROD *takes the record off the player and* ENID *sits.*

VIV *pops her head round the door.*

ENID. Them gone.

VIV (*enters the room*). Thank God for that.

ENID. Where you did go?

VIV. For a walk. It's nice outside.

BROD. You call this weather nice? Well, you was born here.

VIV. Didn't notice the weather. Just walked about, best way to think.

BROD. Walk it out. That's what I always say.

ENID. What you got on you mind you have to walk it out?

The phone rings. VIV *answers.*

VIV. Hello? Who?

BROD. She worried about her exams.

VIV. Call from Jamaica. They want to reverse the charges.

ENID. Bet you a Cynthia.

ENID *takes the phone.*

Hello?

VIV. I been thinking about Jamaica.

ENID. Yes, this is Enid Matthews.

VIV. I want to go out there.

ENID. Yes, I will accept the charges.

BROD. A she? Say hello to her for me.

VIV. I wanna see it for meself.

ENID. You wouldn't survive out there two days by yourself.
Yes, I will hold. (*To* BROD.) I bet you a money she want.

BROD. People back home think Caledonian Road paved with
gold.

ENID. What you think she after this time? House with
swimming pool?

BROD. Or a Rolls-Royce. And a Bentley with real fur and
leather trim.

VIV. There's this volunteer programme. You go out there for a
year and help out where they need you.

ENID (*to* BROD). You see what nonsense you put in the girl
head? (*To* VIV.) What about university? (*To phone*.) Yes, I'm
still here.

VIV. Loads a people take a year off. I can go next year.

ENID. You don't know what it like out there. You don't
understand what poverty do to people. The last time I went
out there they beg me for this, beg me for that, go through
my suitcase when I outta the house, steal my clothes. They
think we have so much. They don't imagine how we live
over here.

VIV. It can't be that bad... Uncle Brod says.

ENID. Brod fill you head with foolishness. You think is some
tropical paradise?

VIV. Mum please.

ENID. Is paradise for rich American tourist. But for the rest of
us... Go to university. Forget about Jamaica. Cynthia? Good
to hear your voice too, Sis.

VIV. Tell her, Brod.

BROD. When you mother ever listen to me?

ENID. What, Cynth? What you say? I can't hear you... Cynthia talk to me, nuh.

As ENID *listens something drains out of her. She drops the phone, but* BROD *catches hold of it and continues the conversation.* ENID *has turned away from* BROD *and* VIV.

VIV. Mum?

BROD. Is Brod, Cynth... When? How she... Yes... Yes...

VIV. Mum.

ENID. Tell her I will wire the money tomorrow.

BROD. We will wire you the money tomorrow... Yes yes we all right, Cynth. You look after youself... Tomorrow, yes, tomorrow.

BROD *puts the phone down.*

ENID (*to* BROD). Have to... Have to look money...

BROD. I sorry, Enid. She was a mother to me as well.

BROD *reaches out to* ENID *but she moves away.*

VIV. I'm sorry.

ENID. Get yourself a drink, Brod.

BROD. You want one?

ENID *shakes her head.*

ENID. Ah lie Cynthia a tell. She jus' want money...

BROD. She nah lie, Enid. Mooma dead.

ENID. No.

BROD. Mooma dead.

Pause.

ENID. A them kill her. Them never look after her properly. All them got 'pon them mind a money.

BROD. Is what you saying, Enid? Mooma was a old woman.

ENID. Then who kill her then? Me?

BROD. Nobody kill her. Her time just come.

ENID starts to leave.

ENID. I want to see her.

VIV. Where you going, Mum?

ENID. Money send money... Send money for Mooma funeral.

BROD. You don't have to do that now, Enid. It can wait.

ENID. No, Brod. Nuttin ever wait.

ENID goes, leaving BROD and VIV.

Scene Four

Very late that night. ENID's living room. ENID sits on the sofa with a drink. The lights are out but the room is lit with the lights from outside. ENID sips her drink. VIV puts her head round the door and looks in, stands in the doorway in her nightdress, watching ENID. ENID picks up her glass again.

VIV. Mum. (*Moves into the room.*) Can't you sleep?

ENID doesn't answer, sips from the glass.

You can't sit here in the dark all night.

ENID. Don't turn the light on.

Pause. VIV watches ENID.

I'm used to sitting in the dark. You think me mother could afford electricity? Hot an' cold running water? Flush toilet? We shower in waterfall.

VIV. That sounds amazing.

ENID. You ever been hungry, Viv?

VIV. Yeah. I've been hungry…

ENID. Not that little nibbling English lunchtime hunger. I talking 'bout the sort that roar in your belly day and night till you think you going mad with the thought a food. You think is easy living off the land? The land fail you, you might as well be dead.

VIV. You don't live off the land any more.

ENID. Oh yes, I did escape didn't I? Lucky me. (*Beat.*) You know where I come from? I come from the dirt. I come from the poorest family in the whole a Jamaica. People used to laugh at us, pick on us. An' we still use to walk around like we was something. (*Laughs at herself, bitter.*) Escape. To what? Where I going run to now?

VIV. Why should you want to run anywhere?

ENID. Sometime I feel like a cat chasing him own tail. Going round and round and getting nowhere but dizzy. (*Slight pause. Deep in thought.*) You think I want to come here? I never want to come here. I wanted to go to America like me uncle.

VIV. I never knew you had an uncle in America.

ENID. I never tell you?

VIV. You never tell us anything.

ENID. Him come back visit with him wife. She was like something out of a film. Straighten she hair an' red up she face. When she leave the house I look in her suitcase. You shoulda see she underclothes – pink an' silky.

VIV. You went through her suitcase?

ENID. Thief a pair a stockings.

VIV (*shocked*). You? Mum!

ENID. She woulda give me if I ask her. But I was too shy. Can you imagine the shame a putting a woman like that in we little wooden shack? Long after them gone I couldn't stop thinking about her. An' America. I cry for days when them say they wasn't taking any more people. (*Beat.*) We have any chocolate tea? I have a taste for a big cup a Mooma chocolate tea.

VIV. I don't know how to make it.

ENID. Chocolate tea and a thick slice a hard dough bread. Old time woman could cook. Roast breadfruit. Callaloo. See Mooma grating chocolate over mortar. 'Come on, girl. Roll it up small. Like little dumpling.'

VIV. I can make you some fried dumpling.

ENID. One day Mooma take me on a long walk. I don't know why. Just tek me to places in the district I never know before. Secret places. Many time you couldn't find Mooma. She must be just sit an' think and dream in them place. Hear Mooma singing... (*Sings snatch of song.*)

VIV. That's a nice song.

ENID. You know, the day I was to leave she never say goodbye to me? Couldn't find her, search everywhere. You know where she was? In the field, working hard like it was jus' any other day, cutting away with she cutlass. 'Mooma,' I say, 'I gone now.' She never turn round, jus' carry on working, chop chop chop, play deaf. In the end I had to give up, walk away. (*Slight pause.*) It wasn't easy to leave. (*Slight pause.*) You want another drink?

VIV *shakes her head and watches her mother as she pours a drink into cup.*

VIV. I don't drink. Neither do you. (*Suddenly noticing something in her mother.*) You drunk, Mum?

ENID. Me? Miss Bible Drawers? (*Laughs.*) A so you father use to call me. Because I din't want to end up like all the other girls in the district. I had plans. I wasn't going to let no blasted man breed me up. (*Sips from the glass, spills some.*)

VIV. You never talk about him.

ENID. You don't remember him?

VIV *shakes her head.*

Every night we douse rags in petrol, light them up for torches then run up Peggy Hill. We sit by we self and plan through the night. We going to be big shots in London. He was a charmer. Everybody in the district love him, put money down buy him a ticket for the ship to England. When I wave him off he say soon as me reach a England I will send for you. Six months pass I don't hear from him. Ten months. Nuttin. He forget me. Exactly a year after him leave I get a airmail letter with a ticket in it. He save every single penny he work to buy that ticket.

VIV. Hope I find someone to love me like that. What happened to you?

ENID *doesn't answer, drains her drink then stands up unsteadily. She looks in a drawer and takes out a small account book.*

ENID. I had was to give you something.

She hands the building society account book to VIV. VIV *takes the book and looks inside.*

VIV. You musta bin saving ages.

ENID. Once I put me mind to something…

VIV. I can't take this.

ENID. You need books and clothes for university.

VIV. I haven't passed the exams yet.

ENID. But you will.

VIV. So, this is a down payment.

ENID. What?

VIV. What if I don't want to go to university? What if I want to travel like you did, fall in love…

ENID. Love has teeth, Viv.

VIV. It's too much. Spend it on yourself.

ENID. What I would buy for myself? High heels? Stockings? I'm not a dreaming sixteen-year-old any more. I'm a big woman.

VIV. What will I spend it on? I never go out except to go to school. Spend my life bent over books that have nothing to do with me. I'm not like you and Del.

ENID (*pressing the book on* VIV). Take it. Take it. Take it. Take it.

VIV. All right. (*Takes the book.*) All right. (*Slight pause.*) I can't live your life for you. I don't know what you want. What do you want?

ENID. I want... I want to go home.

Scene Five

A few weeks later. MAI*'s room. Midday.* MAI *takes cards from a pile on the table and places them face up. She takes up a saucer on which is a heap of salt. She sprinkles salt around the room.* DEL *appears wearing only an outsize T-shirt. She's rubbing her eyes, just woken up.*

DEL. What's going on?

MAI. Sssh.

DEL. You gone mad or what?

MAI. Go back to bed.

> DEL *watches.*

> MAI *continues, self-conscious. She spills the salt.*

See what you done with you evil eye. See how you make me spill it?

DEL. It's only salt.

MAI. Only salt...

DEL. I broken the spell or what?

MAI. I have to start again. (*Mops her brow.*) I getting too old.

DEL. Trying to win back another fugitive husband?

MAI. I said is none a your business.

DEL. Don't know why those women bother.

MAI. You going spend the day naked?

DEL. I only just got up.

MAI. What if somebody call round?

DEL. They come to see you.

MAI. What sort of impression you going give?

DEL. All right. I'll get dressed. (*Beat.*) I couldn't sleep.

MAI. No?

DEL. Those pictures your son put on his wall... I had
    nightmares I was being crushed by a pair a gigantic pink tits.

MAI. He take after my husband.

DEL. Can't imagine you married.

MAI. I done many things you wouldn't think.

DEL. Your husband didn't mind you doing the obeah?

MAI. He had no choice. Neither did I. It was my calling.

DEL. Do you ever talk to him... his spirit?

MAI. That's for me to know.

DEL. Will your son come back?

MAI. When he's ready.

DEL. Can't you use the obeah to find him?

MAI. You can't make a person do anything they don't want to.

DEL. So, how comes you sell love potions?

MAI. Love potions are to make people love themselves. Want some?

DEL. No way.

MAI. So, what you doing poking around my things?

DEL. You'd be shocked if that stuff really worked, wouldn't you?

MAI. You doubt it?

DEL. Don't you?

MAI. Don't tell me we run outta salt. Stop playing with my cards.

DEL. Why? Burn my fingers or something?

MAI. Few nights you been here an' I can't find a damn thing.

DEL. You make it all up, don't you? Come on, I won't tell anyone.

MAI. You think I make it up?

Pause. MAI *takes* DEL*'s hand.*

You have a liking for books, but when you read words run across the page like black ants. The teachers say you slow, so you give up and run with a crowd who make you feel like you belong. At least that's what you used to think, but just recently you have had a change of heart. (*Lets go of* DEL*'s hand.*) If me wrong say me wrong.

DEL (*surprised but not wanting to show it*). Any phoney can take a lucky guess.

MAI. Look, you want to stay here in my house you abide by my rules, y'hear? You got to learn to respect...

DEL. Here we go again. I'll make breakfast.

MAI. Don't turn your back on me, girl!

DEL *turns still shuffling the cards.*

I was talking about respect.

DEL. I need a sermon I'll go to church.

MAI. Don't speak to me like that. You think I'm your mother?

DEL *drops the cards.*

You do that on purpose. This evening you pack you bags and find somewhere else.

DEL. All right. I will.

MAI. An' if any a these missing is me and you.

MAI *stoops to pick up the cards. She has a dizzy spell.* DEL *catches hold of her and walks her over to a chair.*

DEL. Sit down, take it easy.

MAI. Mash up everything you touch.

DEL. I don't mean to spoil things.

MAI. You never think, do you, girl?

Cock crows.

DEL. Shut up.

MAI. They want their breakfast.

DEL *goes over to the cupboard, takes some grain which she puts in an enamel bowl.*

Remember to talk to them. They like it when you talk to them.

DEL. I'm not talking to no chickens.

MAI. Gently. Put some grain in you hand.

DEL *sullenly throws grain out to yard then puts the bowl away.*

DEL. You're not really going to chuck me out, are you?

MAI. Give me a reason why I shouldn't.

DEL *takes* MAI*'s hand.*

DEL. You like having me around. At first you thought I was a bit of a handful, but now you're starting to think that I'm actually quite good company. (*Imitating* MAI.) If me wrong say me wrong.

MAI (*pulling her hand away*). You wrong. When you going to the job centre?

DEL. I've already signed on.

MAI. Is the least you can do. I can't afford to feed the both of us on my little money.

Knock at the door.

What they want with me at this time?

DEL. Probably one of the husbands wants you to get off his back.

MAI. You put on some clothes.

MAI *goes out.* DEL *quickly picks up love potion and dabs some behind her ears.* MAI *returns with* VIV.

VIV. Del.

DEL. What d'you want?

MAI. What a nice way to talk to a visitor. You not going to offer her a cup a tea?

DEL. We run out a tea.

MAI (*puts her hat and coat on*). Don't tell me you drink the last tea bag? Thank God you getting you giro. I can't put up with you eating me outta house and home. What else we need from the shop? Tea, bread, milk...

DEL. And salt.

MAI. Oh yes, salt. (*To* VIV.) Tell her to put on some clothes.

MAI *goes. The sound of the chickens.*

VIV. Do they lay eggs?

DEL. They're just decorative, mostly. But sometimes she uses them in her... you know... obeah. I've seen her.

VIV. Really?

DEL. I see her wring its neck with her bare hands. Poor thing was flapping round the room for an hour with no head, blood everywhere.

VIV. I couldn't stop here with all that going on.

DEL (*laughing*). Your face.

VIV. That's not funny.

DEL. She's harmless.

VIV. What if she requires a fresh young virgin as a human sacrifice? I'd watch meself if I were you.

DEL. Fresh young virgin? That's me out then, ennit?

VIV. You can't have a baby here.

DEL. Why not? Anyway, I'll be out of here soon. Council put you on the top of the list when you're pregnant. I might get a garden.

VIV. That why you did it?

DEL. No, it is not why I DID it. God, Viv.

VIV. I'm not gonna let you have my niece here.

DEL. First I heard aunt's got rights.

VIV. You got milk yet?

DEL. You are such a pervert.

VIV. Wouldn't surprise me if you don't.

DEL. I look after meself.

VIV. Don't look like it. Place smells damp. Be horrible in the winter. Baby'll get fungus on its lungs. (*Beat.*) They're dropping like flies in the sixth form: Sharon Gibbs, Glenna Murphy, Debbie Foster. Debbie Foster was so far gone she couldn't fit the desk in the exam room. Then she had to go to the loo every five minutes.

DEL. Probably had the answers written on her belly.

VIV. How you gonna manage? Baby's gonna need clothes, nappies. I'll help look after it if you come home.

DEL. Let me get on with my life, can't you?

VIV. I want to be there when it comes.

DEL. Hold my hand? Be escaping yourself in – what? – coupla months? You'll be going to wild parties, there'll be sex, drugs, booze. (*Looks* VIV *up and down*.) No, you won't, will you? You're such a good girl.

VIV. I'm not as good as you think.

DEL. Why, what you been up to?

VIV. Wouldn't you like to know? So, what d'you do all day?

DEL. There's loads to do round here. I'm in charge of them chickens. They've all got their own unique personalities.

VIV. What happened with you and Roy?

DEL. I'm finished with men.

VIV. Did you beg?

DEL. No, I did not beg. / What is wrong with you?

VIV. Sharon Gibbs got down on her knees on Oxford Street.

DEL. For God's sake, Viv. He begged me, actually, but I weren't having none of it.

VIV. He called round looking for you. You can imagine what Mum thought about that.

DEL. You better not have told him where I am.

VIV. I ain't told no one. (*Beat.*) What's it feel like?

DEL. You wanna try it? You get sick, you get tired…

VIV (*takes an envelope out of her jacket pocket*). I wanted to give you this.

DEL. What is it? (*Looks inside and sees the cash.*) Where d'you get all this? You got a Saturday job or you taken to crime or what?

VIV *doesn't reply.*

Did the old woman give you this? For being a good girl.

VIV. She told me to give it to you.

DEL. Liar.

VIV. She won't mind, though.

DEL. She'd go mad if she knew you'd given it to me.

VIV. No, she wouldn't. You're her favourite.

DEL. Me? Are you taking the piss?

VIV. You left me all on my own with her. How's that fair?

DEL. Isn't she a bit calmer now that I'm not there?

VIV. S'pose. She's different since her mum... you know... (*Beat.*) Do you think we'd have got on with her mooma?

DEL. Why not? Who knows?

VIV. She was the last of our grandparents. Imagine that, a whole generation gone, and we never met any of them. Never even seen a photograph...

DEL. That's life isn't it? What you doing here anyway? Shouldn't you be sitting some exam?

VIV. 9 a.m. English Literature, Paper One.

DEL. So, you'd better get a move on. You're late.

VIV. I've already been.

DEL. That was quick. You are a clever girl.

VIV. I walked out.

DEL. What?

VIV. My one act of rebellion and I'm shitting myself.

DEL. Why did you do that? Didn't your answers come up?

VIV. Oh, I knew all the answers. Pat me on the head and they all come tumbling out, say exactly what the examiners want to hear. But no matter how hard I search for myself in them books, I'm never there.

DEL. And where's walking out gonna get you? A job in a factory?

VIV. Me and those teachers don't speak the same lingo. Things I feel they haven't got words for. I need another language to express myself.

DEL. Go back to school and sit that exam.

VIV. It's too late. I failed it now.

DEL. You're bright. You'll make up the marks in the next paper.

VIV. I thought you of all people would understand.

DEL. So, you turn bad gyal now? Am I supposed to be impressed? I am not impressed, Viv.

VIV. I always do what everyone else wants me to. From now on I'm gonna do what I want.

DEL. Are you trying to fuck your life up? Get out.

VIV. Oi, what you doing? Are you chucking me out?

DEL. Fuck off out of it, Viv.

VIV. Can't make me.

DEL. Can't I? Can't I?

> DEL *pushes* VIV. *Surprisingly,* VIV *responds by pushing her back. A sisterly tussle ensues and ends with* DEL *taking* VIV *by the collar and dragging her, protesting, to the doorway and throwing her out.*

(*Throwing* VIV*'s bag after her.*) And don't come back unless it's to show me a fucking certificate.

DEL *presses her back against the door as* VIV *pounds on the door then gives up. Silence.*

Scene Six

Evening. MAI*'s bedsit. There's a lighted candle on the table and a glass of water.* ENID *sits at the table with her palm held out.* MAI, *concentrating, holds* ENID*'s palm. Their session is coming to an end.* ENID *seems distracted, lost.*

MAI. You going on a long journey. (*Beat.*) So you better look out you passport. (*Beat.*) I could do with a bit a sunshine meself. (*Beat.*) That will be fifteen pounds.

ENID *rummages in her bag and takes out money, which she hands to* MAI *who puts it away.* ENID *sits, handbag in lap.* MAI *watches her as if waiting for her to do something.*

ENID. My daughter run away from home. Weeks now I haven't seen her.

MAI. They all have to fly the nest sometime. An' a good thing too if you ask me. We don't want them beside us all the day a we life, do we? I was glad when I get me son off me hands. Now I lucky if I get a Christmas card.

ENID. I don't know where she is.

MAI. Rest assured, Enid Matthews. She will be all right. You want a bottle a stout?

ENID. I thought you could give me something, a prayer, some ointment, anything that could protect her.

MAI. Yes, I might have something. Let me look.

ENID. Did I tell you me mother die?

MAI. So did mine. Eighteen years ago now. I still miss her. We don't appreciate them till them gone. Thas what I tell my son.

ENID. Our children are right to blame us. If we can't give them a good life we shouldn't have them.

MAI. For me, a good life is a roof over me head, a good meal every day an' a bottle a cold stout. What you call a good life?

ENID. See you children living life like normal people. Over here the children can't live like normal people.

MAI. You should be proud a you children. Didn't you say the younger one studying for big exam?

ENID. Viv will be all right. They can't take you education away from you. But the bigger one… I worry she a go destroy herself.

MAI. These English children live off them wits.

ENID. She… Two years ago she and her friends go shoplifting, get catch. Police come to my door. Police, Miss Mai. She get a caution, but… the shame.

MAI. It isn't your shame.

ENID. I have to be man and woman, shout so them hear me and when I hear meself I think, why that woman shouting so?

Pause.

(*Taking the hint.*) Sorry I taking up you time. I better go home.

MAI. Don't worry, lady. You take all the time you want.

ENID *seems lost in thought.*

ENID (*smiling*). You have chicken…

MAI. No law against it. If the woman upstairs didn't take out a court order on me. I give her court order. When I set one big duppy 'pon she… Though of course I can't do that. I use my gift only to do good.

ENID. If I did send that money home she wouldna die. Why I din't send them something as soon as I get the letter?

MAI. We all got to go sometime. Is in the book: a time to born, a time to die.

ENID. I was saving up to send for her, but me run outta time.

MAI. You want something else, lady?

Standing, ENID *stares straight ahead, then her face contorts and her mouth opens in a soundless scream. Then the sound comes – a howl of pain, which may have echoes of* BROD*'s talking in tongues in Scene Three.*

Let it out, lady.

ENID *sobs quietly then pulls herself together.*

Feel better ennit?

ENID. Weeks now I ain't sleep.

MAI. Maybe you should see a doctor.

ENID. What doctor know about our illness? Just give you pills to sick you stomach and a doctor certificate. What they know about a black woman soul?

MAI (*understanding*). What you want me to do for you?

ENID. Sometimes I wake up in the middle of the night and I can't move, can't call out. I feel a pressure all round here. Like something sitting on my chest, crush the life outta me. Please. Take this evil spirit off a me.

MAI. If this was back home I woulda say bring me two a you best fowl as a sorta sacrifice. Over here I don't think the blood a two meagre chicken going make you better.

ENID. Is this I come here for? Look at me. (*Smiles, bitter.*) Miss English.

MAI. It not easy to turn you back on one country and start fresh in foreign. It mash up you life. Things happen you wouldn't imagine. When I see them children on the TV, so angry and betrayed… Whuh!

ENID. You ever wonder if it was worth it?

MAI. Their life will be easier. In time. (*Fetches small bottles and gives them to* ENID.) Take these. Make a sign a the cross on you forehead with this one in the morning and this one at night. Pressure soon ease. Soon you notice life picking up again.

ENID (*reaching into her bag*). How much?

MAI. Nuttin. I give as a friend.

ENID. Thank you. Thank you for your help.

> ENID *goes*. MAI *sits down and takes her wig off, blows out the candle*. DEL *enters carrying a jacket*.

MAI. Come here expecting me to give them the answers – palm reading, herbal bath, tricks with cards, read the bumps on their heads – expect me to reach into their souls and stick the broken pieces back together. They have sucked me dry. I've come to the end. My battery dead. Finished. I have had enough.

DEL. I'm going to get some fresh air.

MAI. I want you out of here by Wednesday evening.

DEL. All right.

MAI. I mean it. You should be helping each other to survive. Don't you feel for her?

DEL. She hates me. Always has, ever since I was a little kid. She thinks I'm bad.

MAI. I was hard on my boy. I didn't hate him. I was trying to save him. He used to tell me how he never feel even a little bit British. He used to go on and on at me – in a cockney accent. He would never rest, always dreaming about escape, turning it round and round in him mind. But where the hell he going to escape to? If instead a going round like a madman he could find some peace in himself, journey inside himself, everything would be all right. You at peace with yourself, you at home anywhere.

DEL. How can you love yourself when you're always bottom of the pile?

MAI. I was saying that hate destroys…

DEL. At least hate keeps you fighting.

MAI. But who are you fighting?

DEL. I don't wanna fight you, Mai. I'm grateful for the room.

MAI. Why don't you go home? You mother probably still waiting at the bus stop. Run and catch her up.

DEL. I don't want to.

MAI. You think things would change by now. My grandfather's grandfather come to Jamaica in the hold of a ship. My mother did run away to Cuba in the twenties to cut cane, and I came here. It must be some kinda curse that condemn our people to wander the earth like ghosts who can't find rest. So, now where you going?

DEL *stands for a while as though thinking about it, smiles and shrugs.*

DEL. For a walk.

DEL *goes.*

Scene Seven

MAI*'s living room. Very early the next morning.* BROD *lies stretched out on the table.* DEL *is looking down at him quizzically. She puts her hand to his face, checks his breathing, lifts his hand and lets it flop back. She puts her ear to his chest.* MAI *stands beside her, carrying a mug of water.*

MAI. Him dead?

DEL. Not yet.

MAI. Good.

MAI *tips water from the mug into* BROD*'s face. They watch him as he blinks, then slowly comes to life, groaning. He sits up and blinks, then stares at* DEL *and* MAI.

BROD. This heaven?

DEL. We look like angels, Uncle Brod?

MAI. You know this old tramp?

BROD. Old tramp?

DEL. He's my uncle – family friend. Lives up the road from us and stops by every day for his rice and peas.

BROD. There was no rice and peas last night, I tell you. You mother gone mad. If she din't turn me outta the house.

DEL. Why?

BROD. Say she carry too many people for too long and throw me and Viv out the house.

DEL. Where's Viv?

BROD. She gone to stay with a friend.

DEL. She shoulda come here.

MAI. Here? The landlady think I up to no good in here as it is. She say she ain't see so many people pass through here since Carnival.

BROD. All the years I know her, grow up in the same yard – and she kick me out into the street with nowhere to go.

MAI. So the man must be spend the evening in public house. Then after, come knocking on my door, waking up my neighbours in middle night a shout say how him gone blind.

DEL. Blind?

BROD. If you did drink a bottle a rum to yourself you could see anything?

DEL. When you gonna learn, Uncle Brod?

MAI. Look what him do to me table. Why him have to come here?

BROD. I wanted to speak to my young friend. There was something I had was to tell her.

DEL. What?

BROD. My mind gone blank.

MAI. Minute I set eye 'pon that Enid Matthews I know say the woman was trouble. I did read it in she palm.

BROD. You do reading?

DEL. Palms, cards, tea leaves, you name it, she does it.

MAI. I was thinking a retiring.

BROD. You does heal?

MAI. Only by appointment.

BROD. I can make appointment now?

MAI (*nods at* DEL). See my secretary.

DEL. You what?

BROD. You see, I have this bad back…

MAI. Sunday is my day of rest.

BROD. Oh. (*Rubs his throat.*) I thirsty.

MAI. You want some water?

BROD. I would prefer a –

    MAI *gives him a look.*

    A drop a water would an nice.

    MAI *goes out.*

DEL. Poor Uncle Brod.

BROD. Poor Broderick James. A man condemn to roam the earth from public house to public house in search of that elusive perfect beer.

DEL. You still drunk?

    BROD *holds his head.*

You want an aspirin?

BROD. The pain feel good; I like to pay a penance.

DEL. You drink too much.

BROD. It help me forget.

DEL. What?

BROD (*a revelation to him*). I forget.

DEL. I've heard that joke before.

BROD. You expect a old drunk like me to create new ones?

DEL. You're not an old drunk.

BROD (*looking down at himself and getting down off the table, stretches*). You think you mooma would an' let me back in if I serenade she under she window?

DEL. I'd play it cool if I were you, Brod. (*Beat.*) You love my mum or what?

BROD. What sorta question that?

DEL. Do you?

BROD. Not in that way.

DEL. Why not?

BROD. After everything we been through it hard to find you have any love left. You mother say she finish with love.

DEL. Just wondered…

BROD. Why don't you go and see her? She ain't been right since you leave. She don't clean, she don't cook.

DEL. Poor Uncle Brod missing his ackee and saltfish?

BROD. I can look after meself.

DEL. And so can I.

BROD. That must be why you looking so well. (*Indicates her stomach.*) The father visit you?

DEL. I don't want him to. And what about you, Brod? Do you
see your wife and kids?

BROD. No…

DEL. Why not? (*Beat.*) What makes you men allergic to the
sound of a baby crying?

BROD. I didn't run away. Yes, I went wild for a time, when we
was all young. I made mistakes but that didn't give her the
right to say I couldn't see my kids, take them back to
Jamaica. I yearn for them every day.

DEL. Good old Uncle Brod.

BROD. I wasn't bad as some a these men. Take your father. Now,
he was a madman. I never see a man eyes look so empty. At
first him an' you mother share everything. When one work in
the morning the other one look after the kids and go to work at
night. Them was a good team. I really believe it would work.
It wasn't till we get job a Smithfield meat market that him start
to change. Hear the other men, yah, 'Show us yer tail, yer
black monkey.' Keep our mouth shut, keep our anger inside.
But you father change from a smiling boy into a hard man.
Even him face change to favour a lump a dead meat. He used
to love your mother and now he can't stand her: him come
home from work bitter and tired and the woman a hover round
him smiling and laughing. He can't stand it. He want to wipe
the smile off her face. If they won't treat him like a human
being outside, him make sure she treat him like a king in him
own house: 'Meat raw. Go cook it again. You give big man
food with no salting?' I'm not saying he wouldna do the same
thing if he was back home, what I saying is that coming here
speeden things up because no one care what he want to do to a
black woman. One time I go to the house and he was…

DEL. I don't wanna know.

BROD. You don't want to hear? Why not? Why don't you want to
hear about how you mother get a beating? Because you want to
think of her as a monster? You soon be a mother yourself.

DEL. You come here to tell me this rubbish?

BROD. She never want you and Viv to see anything bad in the house. Thas why she lef' him when you was baby.

DEL. I'll never be a victim.

BROD. She not Nanny a the Maroons.

DEL. Who's Nanny a the Maroons?

BROD. You mother never want me to tell you any a this. Promise me you won't let her know...

MAI *comes in with water.*

MAI. Is you leave the back door open?

BROD. Del?

DEL *(ignores* BROD). Never touched it.

MAI. The chicken them gone.

DEL. They won't have got far. They always come back.

BROD. I gone, then.

MAI. So quick? What about you water?

BROD. I got things to do.

DEL. Like what?

BROD. I might just try to serenade Enid under she window.

BROD *goes.* DEL *walks up and down the room.*

MAI. But what a man mad.

DEL. He's mad all right. You should hear the shit he comes out with.

MAI. Him is a joker, yes.

DEL. The man's one big joke.

DEL *kicks a wall in frustration.*

MAI. Let it out lady.

DEL *is done.*

Feel better, ennit?

DEL. What are you looking at?

MAI. I never notice before how you wide and full between the eyes.

DEL. What's Uncle Brod know anyway? Makes things up when he's drunk. The old girl's tougher than she looks.

MAI (*distracted now*). You frontal lobe big where them meet at the nose root. You know what that mean?

DEL. The man's a fool.

MAI. How I didn't notice that before? What you say? You call me a fool?

DEL. What a fucking phoney.

MAI. No fool like an old fool.

DEL. I'll show him. Why are you staring at me?

MAI. And now I see it plain plain.

DEL (*self-conscious*). Stop staring at me. Stop...

MAI. Cheers.

MAI *drinks the water.*

Scene Eight

MAI*'s living room. A few weeks later. The room is dark. A broom is propped against the table. DEL sits at the table, at the centre of which is a lighted candle. MAI enters quietly from outdoors and watches. DEL stares at the naked flame, chants under her breath. DEL's chanting is louder.*

DEL. Oh, wonderful and bountiful Goddess of Harmony. Bring me money and prosperity. Shine your radiant and benevolent face down on my finances today. Bring me all the riches I desire today. Thank you Vesta for your generous help.

DEL *claps her hands and a small flame appears.*

MAI. What you up to?

DEL *quickly blows out the candle. The room is much tidier than in previous scenes.* DEL *takes up a duster and proceeds to polish the table.*

I hope you ain't using my equipment for your own selfish ends.

DEL. I was just mucking about.

MAI. You muck about in you own time in future.

DEL. This place look clean or what?

MAI (*runs her finger along the table to test for dust*). Not bad.

DEL. First time this place's been cleaned in years. You need a new coat, Mai.

MAI. Why? I like old things.

DEL. So do I.

MAI. Miss Etta call round?

DEL. I gave her two bottles of protection oil and told her to come back next month.

MAI. She pay you?

DEL. She didn't have her purse on her.

MAI. She never have her purse on her. You mustn't let her fool you with that helpless old woman act. It only work if they pay. They have to invest in their own healing. (*Slight pause.*) Did I ever tell you about Pocomania?

DEL. That's when the women dressed in white and tramped round round in a circle. They'd huff and puff until they got high on the spirit. Why don't we have Poco session? I wanna get high on the spirit, man.

MAI. You need wide open spaces.

DEL. We could go on Hampstead Heath.

MAI. You want to end up in jail?

DEL. We wouldn't, would we?

MAI. Didn't they put Pastor Perry in jail for breaking into Highgate Cemetery and sprinkling fowl blood over this Marx man tombstone?

DEL. Serves him right. Silly old fool.

MAI. Yes, the old ways are dying.

DEL. About time too.

MAI. What you doing here if you not keeping them alive?

DEL (*slightly embarrassed, covering*). It's a laugh, ennit? Better than that burger bar. The things people tell you.

MAI. I ever hear you repeating what go on in here to anybody outside this room is me an' you.

DEL. As if I would.

MAI. You sick this morning?

DEL. Bit.

MAI. You never drink the tea I did leave you?

DEL. It's too strong. Only makes me worse.

MAI. It have to get bad before it get better. You expect everything to come to you easy, don't you? (*Picks up candle.*) You use the last a the candle begging Vesta to make you a millionaire?

DEL. I'll go out and get some more in a minute. (*Sweeping.*)

MAI. No time for that now. You got to take your exams.

DEL. What exams?

MAI. Haven't you been watching me, listening to my consultations, reading my books?

MAI *keeps her coat on and sits.*

So, no time like the present. Sit.

DEL *sits*.

You ready?

DEL *shrugs, bemused*.

Clairvoyance and Spiritual Aptitude.

DEL. You what?

MAI. Also known as Psychoscopy. According to De Laurence what is the physical organ of the soul?

DEL (*searches her memory for the answer, then*). The brain!

MAI. Demonology. What charm you would give a client who see a demon in them sleep?

DEL. A filled red pouch and a protection prayer written on parchment.

MAI. Practical: Part A – thought transference. Close your eyes and tell me what you see.

They both close their eyes. DEL *opens hers and takes a peek at* MAI.

(*Eyes still closed.*) Relax, girl. Feel it. It will come to you.

DEL *closes her eyes, strains to 'see'*.

Now, what did you see?

DEL. I'm not sure… A ship? Floating on the sea?

MAI. That will do.

DEL. I got it right? Really?

MAI. Part B: Divination. (*Offers her open palm for* DEL *to read*.) Read.

DEL *stares at* MAI*'s palm, frowning. She struggles to remember what she's been taught like a child learning to read*.

You see everything you need to know in their eyes.

DEL. I can't.

MAI. Can't can't can't is your favourite word. Come on, girl.

DEL concentrates. She feels something like a sudden jolt. She looks up at MAI.

You feel something?

DEL. My heart… Your heart…

They look at each other for a moment, both understanding what she's seen.

MAI. Read, girl.

DEL reads MAI's palm, but is silent.

I'm going on a long journey, I know.

MAI pulls her hand away.

You passed with flying colours. You're a natural.

DEL. But what I saw…

MAI. Never mind what you saw.

DEL. Shouldn't you see a doctor?

MAI. I don't need no doctor. What doctor know about a black woman soul?

DEL. Do I get a certificate?

MAI. We'll see about that. Now, look sharp. We've got a client coming at half past.

DEL. Half past? Why didn't you tell me? (*Takes a cardbox file from the table.*) What's the name?

MAI. You an' your file. I got all the information I need up here. (*Touches her forehead. She searches on the table for something.*) How did you do that thing with the fire?

DEL. Got it from the joke shop down Deptford High Street.

MAI. Never do it again. This is not magic tricks and tomfoolery. This is science.

DEL. All right, Mai.

MAI. Good. (*Beat.*) I want you to see this client.

DEL. Me?

MAI. Is time. You ready.

DEL. On my own?

MAI. I can't always hold your hand.

DEL. I'll screw it up.

MAI. You won't.

> DEL *prepares for the meeting: puts holy water on the table,*
> *lights a candle.*

DEL. Please stay and listen to me.

MAI. I'm going to visit a friend a mine. Make a change to visit
a friend in her living room rather than a cemetery.

DEL. Don't say that, Mai.

MAI. I'm getting on. One day I'll forget everything.

DEL. I can remember for you. I'll look after you.

MAI (*searching around for something*). You're a good girl, but
why you have to move my things?

DEL. Don't you like the place tidy?

MAI. I like to find my things where I leave them.

> MAI *looks under a cushion and finds her notebook.*

An' I suppose you sweep the dirt under the carpet? Here, this
is for you.

> MAI *hands* DEL *the notebook.*

I been writing things down for years.

DEL. What, like magic spells?

MAI. I don't have a daughter to pass them on to. And my son...
well, he isn't interested.

> *A knock on the door.*

Thas you client. She early. I'm going.

DEL. Don't go. (*A huge revelation.*) I'm nervous, Mai.

MAI. You nervous? What happen to big tough Del? You will be all right.

DEL. What if I say the wrong thing? Upset her? You know what I'm like.

MAI. Remember, the healing begins when you look into their eyes. You can do it. Later.

MAI goes. DEL fiddles with the table, then tidies herself up and looks in the mirror. She moves back into centre stage and lays out the cards. Another knock on the door. DEL crosses to open it. The door opens to reveal ENID.

ENID. I have an appointment.

DEL takes a moment then lets ENID into the room.

Place look different.

DEL. I been spring cleaning.

ENID. At home you couldn't boil water.

DEL looks down at her feet.

I never know say daughter a mine would turn obeah woman.

DEL. Would you like a cup a tea?

ENID. No. Thank you.

DEL. Palm or cards?

ENID. Cards.

ENID sits.

DEL shuffles the cards.

DEL puts the pile on the table and indicates for ENID to cut the deck. ENID does so. DEL shuffles again then lays seven cards face up on the table. She examines the cards.

DEL. I see... I see... I see...

DEL *can't speak, the words won't come out. She blows out the candle and stands up from the table.*

Uncle Brod told me about what that man did to you...

ENID. Brod have no business telling you those things.

DEL. He wants me to know who I am.

ENID. Him think knowing what happen in my life going make you understand who you are?

DEL. Why did you have to make a big secret of everything?

ENID. Brod talk too much.

DEL *goes to a cupboard and takes out the envelope that* VIV *gave her.*

DEL. Viv left this behind.

ENID. Keep it. What I have is yours.

DEL. I don't need money.

ENID. No?

DEL. Send it to your family back home. They need it more than me.

ENID. You think so? In a way we poorer than them. Them all in it together. When I was a girl you kill a cow you share it up, everybody in the distric' get a piece. Here, you poor and you by yourself.

DEL. I'm not coming home.

ENID. I just wanted to see you all right.

DEL. How's Viv?

ENID. She packing up to go to university.

DEL. Bet she's excited.

ENID. Black Studies. You ever hear of such a thing?

DEL. When we were kids and you come home off the night shift, you'd come into our room. It was like there was heat and light coming off you. You thought we was asleep and you'd whisper stories into our ears. Then you'd go and we'd have kisses on our cheeks. We could still smell you, warm in the room.

Why don't you like me?

Pause. It isn't easy for ENID *to say what she has to say.*

ENID. Nobody see you, nobody hear you. You could work fifty years with people and they still don't know you name. People walk through you like you not there, push you out the way. All the time you screaming, you screaming inside but nobody come. You don't exist. How you going teach you children that they don't exist? You got to show them how life hard. Mooma never like me. I was everything she never want to be: I was too black, me hair too dry, everything that make you invisible in the world. All the try I try I could never do anything right for her. Even the last time I go home on visit everybody come round say how I look sharp, call me Miss English, say how them proud a me. But not she... She never say a word. Right up to the end she never say a word to me.

Slight pause.

You say I don't see how them treat you out there. I see it. I see it and it make me want to tear the place down. I would chop off my hand if it would help you. But now is up to you. I been fighting too long, Del. I can't fight any more. I want somebody to hold me now. I want to curl up in somebody lap. I want someone to tell me stories to make the sun shine, someone to gather... gather me up and touch my cheek like I was a prize, not a curse, and stroke my hair like Mooma never could.

DEL *has a struggle with herself. Then she makes a decision. She joins* ENID *at the table and takes her mother's hand into both her own and smoothes the palm with her thumbs. She examines the palm for a moment then looks into her mother's eyes. The lights go down as* DEL *begins the reading.*

The End.

A Nick Hern Book

Leave Taking first published in Great Britain in 1989 as a paperback original by Nick Hern Books Limited, The Glasshouse, 49a Goldhawk Road, London W12 8QP, as part of *First Run*

This new edition published in 2018, in association with the Bush Theatre, London

Leave Taking copyright © 1989, 2018 Winsome Pinnock

Winsome Pinnock has asserted her right to be identified as the author of this work

Cover image: Studio Doug
Inside cover: picture of Nada Pinnock-Graham from author's collection

Designed and typeset by Nick Hern Books, London
Printed in the UK by CPI Group (UK) Ltd

A CIP catalogue record for this book is available from the British Library

ISBN 978 1 84842 740 2